# For a super friend

Written by Siân E. Morgan
Illustrated by Juliette Clarke

**EXLEY**

# Finding you

*It doesn't matter when friends come into
your life.
It could be when you are children sharing toys
together or dreaming of becoming pop stars; or
teenagers finding your way into adulthood,
navigating rocky romances together or at a
chance meeting as two middle-aged widows.*

*Sometimes friends seem to be thrown into our
paths, just at the right times.
And sometimes, they were there all along,
it just took us a while to see them.*

*It would have been so easy to have missed each
other, never found each other and gone our
separate ways.
How lucky for me that we didn't!*

IT NEVER CEASES TO AMAZE ME,
THAT OF ALL THE PEOPLE IN THE WORLD,
OF ALL THE DIFFERENT PATHS
WE COULD TAKE, THAT WE MET AT ALL.

*When we met, something just fell into place.*
*I didn't need to know everything about you*
*before I knew that you were special, that you*
*would come to play a great part in my life.*

*Now I can't possibly imagine not knowing you,*
*not having you in my life.*

# Just as you are

*Friends don't compare you to anyone else; they take you just how you are. You don't need to be the most glamorous, dynamic, made up, best dressed person in the world. With a friend, you feel comfortable just being yourself.*

*Somehow friends manage to tell you that your hair looks terrible or your pull-over's awful without hurting your feelings forever.*

change for Zebra dress and it's us !

*Friends are great at listening, even when they've heard the problem a hundred times before. And they're also great at telling you when it's time to stop grumbling and move on.*

le Sujan

*Friends help you to please yourself, not just
bow to other people's needs, to follow your own
path, not just the one that might be planned
out for you.*

# Accepting you
# for what you are...

*It doesn't really matter if you're having a bad hair day, or made a mess of the decorating, or the special recipe you were cooking just blew up, things look a mess... or you look a mess. Because friends see you at your worst as well as your best.*

*Friends see the real you, the one behind the hairstyle, the makeup, the clothes, the work, family and house...* Very true

*And accept you as you are as well as encourage you to be all that you can be, to experiment, to challenge, to overcome those fears and failures.*

*With a friend you feel comfortable just being yourself.*

# Out on the town!

*Friends have a habit of dragging you out even though you tell them you don't want to go. Sometimes, secretly you're glad they persisted.*

*How could you forget those friends who go to the movies with you, even though they've seen it twice before... not to mention those times they spend explaining the plot because you just don't get it or forgot your glasses.* Sorry, just reminds me of us seeing HUM TUM in India and 'Laws of Attraction' — how bad was that? *Only a friend is brave enough to stay on the dance floor with you all night, or kind enough to sit on the sidelines with you when you're exhausted or lose your courage.*

*And of course, friends go out in twos so they can pass toilet roll under doors and stand guard when locks don't work.*

SOMEHOW FRIENDS WHO GO ON HOLIDAY TOGETHER CAN STILL COME HOME ON SPEAKING TERMS, EVEN IF ONE OF YOU FORGOT THE PASSPORTS OR RAN OFF WITH THE GORGEOUS WAITER.

Yeah - holidays aren't great for us, but it's something that after both experiences we're still buddies!

# Endless talk...

*I love to think of all those times we sat around, so engrossed in conversation, so busy putting the world and ourselves to rights, that endless cups of coffee went cold!*

*I love it that someone is on the same wavelength, that we have shared jokes, that someone understands where I'm coming from without a lot of explanations.* — Oh, that is sooo us!

*Sometimes it's just a good old gossip, sometimes it could be you explaining the internet. It could be a worry or a problem that needs solving. Or it could be a secret love affair, or me trying to convince you that you probably haven't failed your exams.*

It never ceases to amaze me how much we can find to talk about! And even if I'm jabbering at a hundred miles an hour, eating cake, using the wrong words somehow you manage to understand me!

You remember our double conversation - when we were on the phone and listening each other at the same time?! Crazy

WHO ELSE WOULD I TALK TO ABOUT LUMPS, BUMPS AND WOBBLY BITS!

# Keeping you young

*You don't have to look very far to see friends of all ages bouncing around like mad fools on space-hoppers, or skipping through crispy leaves in a park when they think no one else is watching.*

*A friend doesn't cringe with embarrassment when you decide to test a skateboard in a shop... they have a go too!*

*And how do friends manage to talk you into leaping about in a leotard in front of a room full of strangers or flapping about in a swimming pool like a drowning duck.*

BEWARE OF ALL THOSE
SENSIBLE LOOKING
FRIENDS… THEY'RE
THE ONES WHO DECIDE
TO GO TOBOGGANING
DOWN YOUR STAIRS
ON YOUR BEST TRAY AT
TWO IN THE MORNING.

# Growing together

When you're being a bit of a dinosaur about something, a friend often tries to keep you up to date.
Sometimes getting to grips with a DVD can be difficult when you've only just got the hang of the microwave or the remote control for the TV.

Friends look at manuals and instructions and then try and translate them into understandable language. Very slowly.
And when you stand there with a very puzzled look on your face for the tenth time, they take a deep breath and try again.

And they have a habit of persisting, even when you say you'll never get the hang of it!
Sometimes, of course, it's the other way round, and it's their turn to be an absolute twit!

*We deal with jobs that wear us down, colleagues that drive us crazy, wayward husbands, children that bring us joy and frustration, exciting times, challenging times. I handle things better, knowing that I can call on you, if I need to.*

GOOD FRIENDS DON'T CARE HOW

MANY TIMES YOU REINVENT YOURSELF,

JUST SO LONG AS YOU'RE HAPPY.

# Keeping you going...

*Great friends pick up the teacloth when you're doing the dishes, they look for the other spade when you're digging the garden, they hold the soaking wet baby while you run for a towel.*

*If your hairstyle is awful they tell you your earrings are fantastic.* — 'Course your hair always look great; not sure about earrings though!

THEY DON'T JUST CHEER FROM THE SIDELINES, THEY RUN THE RACE WITH YOU AND TELL YOU YOU'RE NEARLY THERE.

# A FRIEND HELPS YOU FIND YOUR GET-UP-AND-GO... ...AND BRINGS IT BACK.

*Sometimes you don't feel very brave on your own, but together you don't think there's anything you can't tackle. The nicest thing is when you're dreading a heartbreaking change and you know you won't have to face it alone. Whenever you worry about tackling something on your own, you can think of your friend and suddenly feel much more brave.*
*Suddenly it doesn't seem quite so scary.*

# Shopping sprees!

*You can always tell when friends are out shopping... They're the ones collapsing with laughter in the dressing rooms, trying on silly hats*

*Or pointing out that you've already got hundreds of pairs of shoes that never see daylight... and you really don't need that red pair that hurt your feet and don't fit properly... even if they are gorgeous and are a bargain.*

*Only a friend could convince you to buy something that you wouldn't usually wear... and be right. And you can always rely on a friend to tell you that your bottom really does look big in those trousers.*

FRIENDS ARE THOSE RARE BREED OF PEOPLE
WHO VISIT SHOPS THEY HATE, JUST FOR YOU.
ONLY A FRIEND WOULD LET YOU DRAG
THEM AROUND THE SHOPS FOR HOURS
WITHOUT COMPLAINING (MUCH!)

# Staying in

Friends mean you don't always have to go out to have fun.

And unexpected visits give you a great excuse to stop tidying and have some fun.

*or painting my house!*

Whether it's putting up those shelves, or helping you forget the guy who just left you or dying your hair (and the bath)...

You can never make a fool of yourself in front of a friend... even if you look like you've just dipped your face in a mud bath, or have huge slices of cucumber stuck to your eyelids.

And you know you can trust them not to tell anyone about dancing around the kitchen table to Tom Jones!

FRIENDS ARE JUST AS HAPPY TO CURL UP
ON THE SOFA IN A PAIR OF OLD
PYJAMAS TO WATCH A WEEPY MOVIE
WITH A HUGE BAR OF CHOCOLATE.

# Trusting you

*I love it that you know parts of me that otherwise wouldn't see the light of day. That you know thoughts of mine that otherwise would remain buried forever. You know things about me that I wouldn't dare tell another living soul for fear they'd fall about laughing or look at me as if I was crazy.*

*You remind me that I am capable. That I can learn a new language or wire a plug without blowing up the house... if I want to. And I can live on my own, fight that disease, manage children or move job... if I ever need to.*

*My life is better for knowing I can confide in you.*

GREAT FRIENDS
ARE THOSE PEOPLE YOU TRUST
WITH THINGS OF EXTRA
SPECIAL VALUE... YOUR BEST
EARRINGS, YOUR MAN,
AND YOUR MOST GUARDED
SECRETS AND FEARS.

GREAT FRIENDS LISTEN
TO YOUR INSECURITIES AND
SHOOT THEM DOWN IN
FLAMES ONE BY ONE.

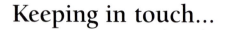

# Keeping in touch...

*Like when I was
dying in Kerala!*

*Somehow friends stay in touch despite hundreds,
even thousands of miles. It can be class changes,
house moves or chaotic lives.*

*The great thing about friends is that geography
won't ever make a difference.*

*Even if you do end up with huge phone bills!*

*Friends stay in your thoughts, whether they
live just around the corner or at the other end
of the world.*

*And it never seems to matter when you see
each other.*

*Sometimes it's enough to talk on the phone or scribble a quick letter or send a funny email to bring back special memories.*
*It could be a postcard that lands on the doormat, a TV show that made you both laugh, or a crazy photo of the last time you met.*

*Sometimes you can go for ages without seeing each other, yet when you meet, it's like you've never been apart, like nothing has changed between you at all. You always manage to pick up exactly where you left off.*

# Just being there for you...

*You never forget a friend who rushes over at two in the morning because there's been an accident, or a friend who sits by your side in the dentists because they didn't want you to go by yourself, who flees the doctors waiting room with you in relief after persuading you that you really don't need that facelift.*

*You always remember a friend that lends you their best shirt even if it's new and who's brave enough to visit when you're spluttering germs everywhere.* — like after my septoplasty!

*And you will always remember the person who you rely on to tell you that you didn't want to work there anyway, when you don't get that job.*